Masonic Symbolism of the Apron & the Altar

By
Albert G. Mackey, William Harvey, H. L. Haywood,
Joseph Fort Newton, J. George Gibson
and H. A. Kingsbury

Copyright © 2019 Lamp of Trismegistus. All rights reserved. No part of this publication may be reproduced or transmitted in any form or by any means, electronic or mechanical, including photocopying, recording, or by any information storage and retrieval system, without permission in writing from Lamp of Trismegistus. Reviewers may quote brief passages.

ISBN: 978-1-63118-428-4

Foundations of Freemasonry
Series

Other Books in this Series and Related Titles

Royal Arch, Capitular and Cryptic Masonry
by William F. Kuhn, William Potts George, High McCurdy and Arthur Edward Waite (978-1-63118-425-3)

Ancient Mysteries and Secret Societies by Manly P. Hall
(978-1-63118-410-9)

Ancient Egyptian Mysteries and Hieroglyphics, Modern Freemasonry & Initiation of the Pyramid by Henry Ridgely Evans, Manly P. Hall, George Smtih and Albert G. Mackey (978-1-63118-430-7)

The Lost Keys of Freemasonry or The Secret of Hiram Abiff
by Manly P. Hall (978-1-63118-427-7)

The Book of Parables by Enoch (978-1-63118-429-1)

Symbolism of the Corner Stone, the North East Corner and the Religious & Masonic Symbolism of Stones by Albert G. Mackey, William Harvey and William Wynn Westcott (978-1-63118-412-3)

Rosicrucian and Masonic Origins by Manly P. Hall
(978-1-63118-000-2)

The Philosophy of Masonry in Five Parts by Roscoe Pound
(978-1-63118-004-0)

The Story and Legend of Hiram Abiff by William Harvey, Manly P. Hall and Albert G. Mackey (978-1-63118-411-6)

Symbolism and Discourses on the Entered Apprentice, Fellowcraft and Master Mason Blue Lodge Degrees
by H. L. Haywood, Asahel W. Gage, William Harvey, Albert G. Mackey and Arthur Edward Waite (978-1-63118-413-0)

Audio Versions are also Available on Audible and iTunes

Table of Contents

Introduction…7

The Apron
by H. L. Haywood…9

The Masonic Apron
by Joseph Fort Newton…19

The Rite of Investiture
by Albert G. Mackey…23

The Apron
by H. A. Kingsbury…31

Symbolism in the Apron
by J. George Gibson…35

The Altar of Freemasonry
by William Harvey…41

The Altar
by H. L. Haywood…53

Introduction

From the beginning of Modern Freemasonry's birthdate of 1717, the intelligentsia of humanity have found refuge for safe reflection within the walls of the fraternity. Masonic writers have produced a nearly incalculable amount of written musings on a multitude of esoteric and philosophical subjects, as they relate to the ancient mysteries that Freemasonry currently storehouses. Sadly, most of it appears to have sat largely unread, as American Freemasonry in particular, continues to transform itself into something that bears little resemblance to what it was originally designed to be. The true essence of Freemasonry is not that of blind patriotism or a single-minded national religion but one of Universal Brotherhood and altruism, designed for the betterment not just of its members but of society as a whole. In particular, for those who are not members of the fraternity, as Freemasonry has always acted as a beacon, to help guide humanity through darker times, with the hopes that one day we will collectively reach a truly enlightened age.

It's not uncommon for new members joining the fraternity to find little education within the walls of many modern lodges, in spite of so much written material available to the membership. Many older members are not simply uneducated with regards to real Masonic history and symbology, not to mention the vast arena of related subjects, but they are disinterested in all of it, as well.

Lamp of Trismegistus is doing its part to help preserve humanity's Masonic history by making some of these classics available to those students who are seeking to unearth the knowledge of these ancient colossi. As such, Lamp of Trismegistus offers its readers highlights of Masonic study, culled from a variety of authors and viewpoints, with the hope bringing education back into the fraternity. So, be sure to check out other titles in our *Foundations of Freemasonry Series* as well as our *Esoteric Classics*, *Theosophical Classics*, *Occult Fiction* and our *Christian Apocrypha Series*, and don't be afraid to let a little altruism into your own heart or even into your Lodge. You can also download the audio versions of most of these titles from iTunes or Audible.

The Apron

by H. L. Haywood

Having been privileged to read a great deal of Masonic literature we may say that on no other one symbol has so much nonsense been written. It has been made to mean a thousand and one things, from the fig leaf worn by Adam and Eve to the last mathematical theory of the Fourth Dimension; and there is little to cause wonder that the intelligent have been scandalized and common men bewildered. If an interpretation can be made that steers a safe course between the folly of the learned and the fanaticism of the ignorant it will have some value, whatever may be said of its own intrinsic worth. Warned by the many who have fallen into the pit of unreason we shall be wise to walk warily and theorize carefully.

Speaking generally, and without the slightest hint of disrespect of our fellow workers in this field, it may be said that a majority of the wildest theories have been based on the shape of the Apron, a thing of comparatively recent origin and due to a mere historical accident. The body of it, as now worn, is approximately square in shape and thus has suggested the symbolism of the square, the right-angle and the cube, and all arising therefrom; its flap is triangular and this has suggested the symbolism of the triangle, the Forty-seventh Proposition, and the pyramid; the descent of the flap over the body of the Apron has also given rise to reasonings equally ingenious. By this method of interpretation men have read into it all manner of things, the mythology of the Mysteries, the metaphysics of

India, the dream-walking of the Kabbalah, and the Occultism of Magic. Meanwhile it has been forgotten that the Apron is a Masonic symbol and that we are to find out what it is intended to mean rather than what it may, under the stress of our lust for fancifulness, be made to mean. When the Ritual is consulted, as it always deserves to be, we find that it treats the Apron (1) as an inheritance from the past, (2) as the Badge of a Mason, (3) as the emblem of innocence and sacrifice.

1. The Apron is an inheritance from the past.

For one purpose or another, and in some form, the Apron has been used for three or four thousand years. In at least one of the Ancient Mysteries, that of Mithras, the candidate was invested with a white Apron. So also was the initiate of the Essenes, who received it during the first year of his membership in that order, and it is significant that many of the statues of Greek and Egyptian gods were so ornated, as may still be seen. Chinese secret societies, in many cases, also used it, and the Persians, at one-time, employed it as their national banner. Jewish prophets often wore Aprons, as did the early Christian candidates for baptism, and as ecclesiastical dignitaries of the present day still do. The same custom is found even among savages, for, as Brother J. G. Gibson has remarked, "*wherever the religious sentiment remains-- even among the savage nations of the earth--there has been noticed the desire of the natives to wear a girdle or Apron of some kind.*"

From all this, however, we must not infer that our Masonic Apron has come to us from such sources, though, for all we know, the early builder may have been influenced by those ancient and universal customs. The fact seems to be that the Operative Masons used the Apron only for the practical purpose of protecting the clothing, as there was need in labor so rough. It was nothing more than one item of the workman's necessary equipment as is shown by Brother W. H. Rylands, who found an Indenture of 1685 in which a Master contracted to supply his Apprentice with "sufficient wholesome and competent meat, drink, lodging and Aprons."

Because the Apron was so conspicuous a portion of the Operative Mason's costume, and so persistent a portion of his equipment, it was inevitable that Speculatives should have continued its use for symbolical purposes. The earliest known representatives of these, we are informed by Brother J. F. Crowe, who was one of the first of our scholars to make a thorough and scientific investigation of the subject (*A.Q.C. vol. V, p. 29*), "*is an engraved portrait of Anthony Sayer. . . Only the upper portion is visible in the picture, but the flap is raised, and the Apron looks like a very long leathern skin. The next drawing is in the frontispiece to the Book of Constitutions, published in 1723, where a brother is represented as bringing a number of Aprons and gloves into the Lodge, the former appearing of considerable size and with long strings.*" In Hogarth's cartoon, "Night," drawn in 1737, the two Masonic figures, Crowe points out in another connection (*See his "Things a Freemason Should Know"*) "have Aprons reaching to their ankles." But other plates of the same period show Aprons reaching only to the knee, thus marking the beginning of that process of shortening, and of general decrease in size and change in shape, which finally gave us the Apron of the present day; for since the garment no longer serves as a means of protection it has been found wise to fashion it in a manner more convenient to wear, nor is this inconsistent with its original Masonic significance. It is this fact, as I have already suggested, that has made the present form of the Apron a result of circumstances, and proves how groundless are interpretations founded on its shape.

According to Blue Lodge usages in the United States the Apron must be of unspotted lambskin, 14 to 16 inches in width, 12 to 14 inches in depth, with a flap descending from the top some 3 or 4 inches. The Grand Lodge of England now specifies such an Apron as this for the First Degree, but requires the Apron of the Second Degree to have two sky-blue rosettes at the bottom, and that of the Third Degree to have in addition to that a sky-blue lining and edging not more than two inches deep, "and an additional rosette on the fall or flap, and silver tassels." Grand officers are permitted to use other ornaments, gold embroidery, and, in some cases, crimson edgings. All the evidence goes to show that these ornate Aprons are of recent origin. The Apron should always be worn outside the coat.

2. The Badge of a Mason.

"The thick-tanned hide, girt around him with throngs, wherein the Builder builds, and at evening sticks his trowel," was so conspicuous a portion of the costume of the Operative Mason that it became associated with him in the public mind, and thus gradually evolved into his badge; for a badge is some mark voluntarily assumed as the result of established custom whereby one's work, or station, or school of opinion, may be signified.

Of what is the Mason's badge a mark? Surely its history permits but one answer to this--it is the mark of honorable and conscientious labor, the labor that is devoted to creating, to constructing rather than to destroying or demolishing. As such, the Mason's Apron is itself a symbol of a profound change in the attitude of society toward work, for the labor of hand and brain, once despised by the great of the earth, is rapidly becoming the one badge of an honorable life. If men were once proud to wear a sword, while leaving the tasks of life to slaves and menials, if they once sought titles and coats of arms as emblems of distinction, they are now, figuratively speaking, eager to wear the Apron, for the Knight of the present day would rather save life than take it, and prefers, a thousand times over, the glory of achievement to the glory of title or name. Truly, the rank has become *the guinea's stamp, and a man's a man for all that*, especially if he be a man that can do; and the real modern king, as Carlyle was always contending, is "the man who can."

If this is the message of the Apron, none has a better right to wear it than a Mason, if he be a real member of the Craft, for he is a knight of labor if ever there was one. Not all labor deals with things. There is a labor of the mind, and of the spirit, more arduous, often, and more difficult, than any labor of the hands. He who dedicates himself to the cleaning of the Augean stables of the world, to the clearing away of the rubbish that litters the paths of life, to the fashioning of building stones in the confused quarries of mankind, is entitled, more than any man, to wear the badge of toil!

3. An Emblem of Innocence and Sacrifice.

When the Candidate is invested with the garment he is told that it is an emblem of innocence. It is doubtful if Operative Lodges ever used it for such a symbolic purpose, though they may have done so in the Seventeenth Century, after Speculatives began to be received in greater numbers. The evidence indicates that it was after the Grand Lodge era, and in consequence of the rule that the Apron should be of white lambskin, that Masons began to see in its color an emblem of innocence and in its texture a suggestion of sacrifice.

In so doing they fell into line with ancient practices for of old, white "has been esteemed an emblem of innocence and purity." Among the Romans an accused person would sometimes put on a garment of white to attest his innocence, white being, as Cicero phrased it, "most acceptable to the gods." The candidate in the Mysteries and among the Essenes were similarly invested, and it has the same meaning of purity and innocence in the Bible which promises that though our sins be as scarlet they shall be white as snow. In the early Christian church the young catechumen (or convert) robed himself in white in token of his abandonment of the world and his determination to lead a blameless life. But there is no need to multiply instances, for each of us feels by instinct that white is the natural symbol of innocence.

Now it happens that "innocence" comes from a word meaning "to do no hurt" and this may well be taken as its Masonic definition, for it is evident that no grown man can be innocent in the sense that a child is, which really means an ignorance of evil. The innocence of a Mason is his gentleness, his chivalrous determination to do no moral evil to any person, man, or woman, or babe; his patient forbearance of the crudeness and ignorance of men, his charitable forgiveness of his brethren when they willfully or unconsciously do him evil; his dedication to a spiritual knighthood in behalf of the values and virtues of humanity by which alone man rises above the brute, and the world is carried forward on the upward way.

It is in token of its texture--lambskin--that we find in the Apron the further significance of sacrifice, and this also, it seems, is a symbolism developed since 1700. It has been generally believed until recently that the Operatives used only leather Aprons, and this was doubtless the case in early days, but Crowe has shown that many of the oldest Lodge records evidence a use of linen as well. "In the old Lodge of Melrose," he writes, "*dating back to the Seventeenth Century, the Aprons have always been of linen, and the same rule obtained in 'Mary's Chapel' No. 1, Edinburgh, the oldest Lodge in the world; whilst Brother James Smith, in his history of the old Dumfries Lodge, writes, 'on inspecting the box of Lodge 53, there was only one Apron of kid or leather, the rest being of linen!' As these Lodges are of greater antiquity than any in England, I think a fair case is made out for linen, versus leather, originally.*"

It can not be said, however, that Brother Crowe has entirely made out his case, for other authorities contend that the builders who necessarily handled rough stone and heavy timbers must have needed a more substantial fabric than linen or cotton. But in any event, the Fraternity has been using leather Aprons for these two centuries, though cotton cloth is generally substituted for ordinary lodge purposes, and it is in no sense far-fetched to see in the lambskin a hint of that sacrifice of which the lamb has so long been an emblem.

But what do we mean by sacrifice? To answer this fully would lead us far afield into ethics and theology, but for our present purpose, we may say that the Mason's sacrifice is the cheerful surrender of all that is in him which is un-Masonic. If he has been too proud to meet others on the level he must yield up his meanness; if he has been guilty of corrupting habits they must be abandoned, else his wearing of the Apron be a fraud and a sham.

Carrying with it so rich a freightage of symbolism the Apron may justly be considered "more ancient than the Golden Fleece or Roman Eagle, more honorable than the Star and Garter," for these badges were too often nothing more than devices of flattery and the insignia of an empty name. The Golden Fleece was an Order of Knighthood founded by Philip, Duke of Burgundy on the occasion of his marriage to the Infanta Isabella of Portugal in 1429 or 1430. It used a Golden Ram for its badge and the motto inscribed on its jewel was "wealth, not servile labor!" The Romans of old bore an eagle on their banners to symbolize magnanimity, fortitude, swiftness and courage. The Order of the Star originated in France in 1350, being founded by John II in imitation of the Order of the Garter; of the last named Order it is difficult to speak, as its origin is clothed in so much obscurity that historians differ, but it was as essentially aristocratic as any of the others. In every case, the emblem was a token of aristocratic idleness and aloofness, the opposite of that symbolized by the

Apron; and the superiority of the latter over the former is too obvious for comment.

The Masonic Apron

by Joseph Fort Newton

Horace Greeley used to say that he would not give a cent for a man who could not spell a word in more than one way - it showed a lack of versatility and inventive genius. Much the same may be said of Masonic symbolism, which is as flexible as it is suggestive, and may be interpreted in many ways, by each initiate or student according to his light. "Each sees what he carries in his heart," as we read in the Prologue of Faust. All of which is brought to mind by a passage in the valuable book, "*True Principles of Masonry*," in which the author tells us, out of a rich and thoughtful mind, what the Apron means to him. It symbolizes that plan for the redemptive making of personality, which Masonry has sought to promulgate from the remotest ages. As we may read:

> "*This apron is composed of a square, surmounted by a triangle, or of seven lines, four in the square and three in the triangle. The lower line in the square, to me, represents selfishness, the lowest and most degrading of all human passions. It has been the common saying, from time immemorial, that 'The love of money is the root of all evil.' But I say to you that selfishness is the root of all evil, because selfishness, in its very worst form, may be entirely free from love of money; that selfishness of Creed and Dogma, that is not willing to concede to another the same freedom of thought, speech and conscience that we demand for ourselves. Selfishness is tie progenitor of all the base passions of the human heart, vanity, deceit, cruelty,*

envy, jealousy, intolerance, greed, malevolence, lust, inhumanity, and brutality.

Rising from this low plane of selfishness, we have two perpendicular lines; the one I call Intellectuality, and the other Spirituality. The one might possibly be termed an attribute of the mind, the other of the soul; and each of them capable of development, independent of, or to the exclusion of the other. For example, a man may have reached the summit of all human knowledge. He may have the intellectual ability of a Euclid or a Sir Isaac Newton, but at the same time be wholly lacking in spirituality, or that faculty of his nature may be wholly dormant. In that case, endowed with the most brilliant intellect that can be conceived of, he may be a moral degenerate.

On the other hand, another man's spirituality may be abnormally developed, to the utter exclusion of intellectuality; in such case you find the religious fanatic or a religious monomaniac.

So we are forced to the conclusion that in order to secure good work, true work and square work - just such work as is needed in the construction of a well-proportioned temple, the development must proceed along both lines of intellectuality and spirituality, in due proportion and harmony with each other. The top line of the Apron's square represents faith - a logical, reasoning faith that has grown up out of, and been projected from, the two lives of intellectuality and Spirituality. A faith that satisfies the longings of my spiritual nature, and at the same time meets with the approval of my reasoning faculties.

Parallel with the top line of the Apron's square, and in close proximity to it, is the line at the base of the triangle. To me it represents unselfishness and self-sacrifice. Rising from this line are the two converging lines of the triangle; the one love of God, and the other love of my fellow man; and their intersection at the apex of the triangle generates the great undying light of Freemasonry."

Whether or not all will accept that interpretation of the symbolism of the Apron, all will agree that it is wise and good and inspiring teaching, which every man of us ought to lay to heart as the years come and go, like hooded figures, each bringing its quota of joy and sorrow, and also its opportunity for advancement toward that coronation of character which is the crown of life and the defeat of death. So mote it be.

The Rite of Investiture

by Albert G. Mackey

Another ritualistic symbolism, of still more importance and interest, is the rite of investiture. The rite of investiture, called, in the colloquially technical language of the order, the ceremony of clothing, brings us at once to the consideration of that well-known symbol of Freemasonry, the Lamb-Skin Apron.

This rite of investiture, or the placing upon the aspirant some garment, as an indication of his appropriate preparation for the ceremonies in which he was about to engage, prevailed in all the ancient initiations. A few of them only it will be requisite to consider.

Thus in the Levitical economy of the Israelites the priests always wore the abnet, or linen apron, or girdle, as a part of the investiture of the priesthood. This, with the other garments, was to be worn, as the text expresses it, "for glory and for beauty," or, as it has been explained by a learned commentator, "as emblematical of that holiness and purity which ever characterize the divine nature, and the worship which is worthy of him."

In the Persian Mysteries of Mithras, the candidate, having first received light, was invested with a girdle, a crown or mitre, a purple tunic, and, lastly, a white apron.

In the initiations practiced in Hindostan, in the ceremony of investiture was substituted the sash, or sacred zennaar, consisting of a cord, composed of nine threads twisted into a knot at the end, and hanging from the left shoulder to the right hip. This was, perhaps, the type of the masonic scarf, which is, or ought to be, always worn in the same position.

The Jewish sect of the Essenes, who approached nearer than any other secret institution of antiquity to Freemasonry in their organization, always invested their novices with a white robe.

And, lastly, in the Scandinavian rites, where the military genius of the people had introduced a warlike species of initiation, instead of the apron we find the candidate receiving a white shield, which was, however, always presented with the accompaniment of some symbolic instruction, not very dissimilar to that which is connected with the masonic apron.

In all these modes of investiture, no matter what was the material or the form, the symbolic signification intended to be conveyed was that of purity.

And hence, in Freemasonry, the same symbolism is communicated by the apron which, because it is the first gift, which the aspirant receives--the first symbol in which he is instructed--has been called the "badge of a mason." And most appropriately has it been so called; for, whatever may be the future advancement of the candidate in the "Royal Art," into whatever deeper arcana his devotion to the mystic institution or his thirst for knowledge may carry him, with the apron--his first investiture--he never parts. Changing, perhaps, its form

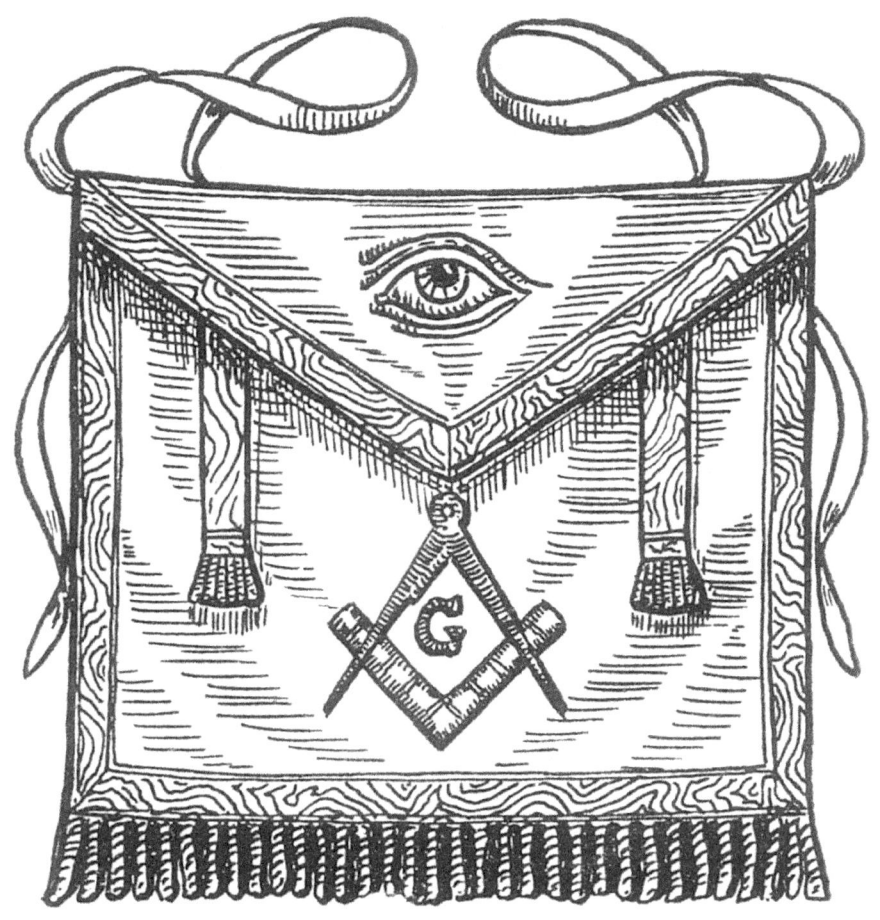

and its decorations, and conveying at each step some new and beautiful allusion, its substance is still there, and it continues to claim the honorable title by which it was first made known to him on the night of his initiation.

The apron derives its significance, as the symbol of purity, from two sources--from its color and from its material. In each of these points of view it is, then, to be considered, before its symbolism can be properly appreciated.

And, first, the color of the apron must be an unspotted white. This color has, in all ages, been esteemed an emblem of innocence and purity. It was with reference to this symbolism that a portion of the vestments of the Jewish priesthood was directed to be made white. And hence Aaron was commanded, when he entered into the holy of holies to make an expiation for the sins of the people, to appear clothed in white linen, with his linen apron, or girdle, about his loins. It is worthy of remark that the Hebrew word LABAN, which signifies to make white, denotes also to purify; and hence we find, throughout the Scriptures, many allusions to that color as an emblem of purity. "Though thy sins be as scarlet," says Isaiah, "they shall be white as snow;" and Jeremiah, in describing the once innocent condition of Zion, says, "Her Nazarites were purer than snow; they were whiter than milk."

In the Apocalypse a white stone was the reward promised by the Spirit to those who overcame; and in the same mystical book the apostle is instructed to say, that fine linen, clean and white, is the righteousness of the saints.

In the early ages of the Christian church a *white garment* was always placed upon the catechumen who had been recently baptized, to denote that he had been cleansed from his former sins, and was thenceforth to lead a life of innocence and purity. Hence it was presented to him with this appropriate charge: "Receive the white and undefiled garment, and produce it unspotted before the tribunal of our Lord Jesus Christ, that you may obtain immortal life."

The *white alb* still constitutes a part of the vestments of the Roman church, and its color is said by Bishop England "to excite to piety by teaching us the purity of heart and body which we should possess in being present at the holy mysteries."

The heathens paid the same attention to the symbolic signification of this color. The Egyptians, for instance, decorated the head of their principal deity, Osiris, with a white tiara, and the priests wore robes of the whitest linen.

In the school of Pythagoras, the sacred hymns were chanted by the disciples clothed in garments of white. The Druids gave white vestments to those of their initiates who had arrived at the ultimate degree, or that of perfection. And this was intended, according to their ritual, to teach the aspirant that none were admitted to that honor but such as were cleansed from all impurities, both of body and mind.

In all the Mysteries and religious rites of the other nations of antiquity, the same use of white garments was observed.

Portal, in his "Treatise on Symbolic Colors," says that "*white, the symbol of the divinity and of the priesthood, represents divine wisdom; applied to a young girl, it denotes virginity; to an accused person, innocence; to a judge, justice*;" and he adds--what in reference to its use in Masonry will be peculiarly appropriate--that, "*as a characteristic sign of purity, it exhibits a promise of hope after death*." We see, therefore, the propriety of adopting this color in the masonic system as a symbol of purity. This symbolism pervades the whole of the ritual, from the lowest to the highest degree, wherever white vestments or white decorations are used.

As to the material of the apron, this is imperatively required to be of lamb-skin. No other substance, such as linen, silk, or satin, could be substituted without entirely destroying the symbolism of the vestment. Now, the lamb has, as the ritual expresses it, "been, in all ages, deemed an emblem of innocence;" but more particularly in the Jewish and Christian churches has this symbolism been observed. Instances of this need hardly be cited. They abound throughout the Old Testament, where we learn that a lamb was selected by the Israelites for their sin and burnt offerings, and in the New, where the word lamb is almost constantly employed as synonymous with innocence. "*The paschal lamb*," says Didron, "*which was eaten by the Israelites on the night preceding their departure, is the type of that other divine Lamb, of whom Christians are to partake at Easter, in order thereby to free themselves from the bondage in which they are held by vice.*" The paschal lamb, a lamb bearing a cross, was, therefore, from an early period, depicted by the Christians as referring to Christ crucified, "that spotless Lamb of God, who was slain from the foundation of the world."

The material, then, of the apron, unites with its color to give to the investiture of a mason the symbolic signification of purity. This, then, together with the fact, which I have already shown, that the ceremony of investiture was common to all the ancient religious rites, will form another proof of the identity of origin between these and the masonic institution.

This symbolism also indicates the sacred and religious character which its founders sought to impose upon Freemasonry, and to which both the moral and physical qualifications of our candidates undoubtedly have a reference, since it is with the masonic lodge as it was with the Jewish church, where it was declared that "no man that had a blemish should come nigh unto the altar;" and with the heathen priesthood, among whom we are told that it was thought to be a dishonor to the gods to be served by any one that was maimed, lame, or in any other way imperfect; and with both, also, in requiring that no one should approach the sacred things who was not pure and uncorrupt.

The pure, unspotted lamb-skin apron is, then, in Masonry, symbolic of that perfection of body and purity of mind which are essential qualifications in all who would participate in its sacred mysteries.

The Apron

By H. A. Kingsbury

But few, if any, of the various symbols regarding which the Masonic candidate is instructed, carry with them a wealth of symbolic significance and interesting suggestion equal to that born by that symbol which the candidate is given, and concerning which he is instructed, in his first degree--the Masonic Apron. The briefest study of its origin, its color, its material, and its shape, and of the various positions in which it is worn, cannot fail to give the student a better realization of the wonderful completeness and perfection of Masonic Symbolism.

The rite of investiture and the significance of that rite (*i.e., the appropriate preparation of the candidate for the ceremonies in which he is about to engage*), come to us from far back in the world's history, and they come "well recommended." The priests of the Israelites wore a linen apron. In the Persian Mysteries the candidate was invested with an apron. The Essenes always provided their novices with robes. And in the Scandinavian Rites the candidate received a shield.

In each of these instances the color of the investiture was, like that of the Masonic apron, white. The significance of that color has always been the same-- purity. That white is the symbol of purity could be illustrated by almost innumerable examples. Throughout the Scriptures are many illustrative references. The Egyptians decorated the head of their principal deity, Osiris, with a white tiara. The disciples of Pythagoras, in attendance at his school, wore garments of white when chanting the sacred hymns. In the early ages of the Christian Church a white garment was placed upon the recently baptized convert to denote that he had been cleansed of his former sins. Portal in his "Treatise on Symbolic Colors" refers to white as "a characteristic sign of purity."

The material of the apron--lambskin--is also of symbolic significance. The ritual states that the lamb has been, in all ages, an emblem of innocence. Examples of the truth of this statement are too common to call for notice here.

The significance of the shape of the apron can be, perhaps, best seen when this symbol is spread to its greatest extent, as illustrated in solid lines in the figure. In this position it leads to the contemplation of the Triangle, the Square, the Nine Significant Numbers, the Broached Thurnel, and the obelisks of

Egypt. That it, by its flap, presents the Triangle, and, by its body, presents the Square, is obvious.

It presents one large figure, composed of two smaller figures, one having three sides and the other four sides; it is bounded by five lines and has six lines in all; the square has four angles and the triangle has three, making seven in all; it may be considered as a full front view of a solid (*a side and a top face of which are indicated by dotted lines in the figure*) composed of a cube surmounted by a rectangular pyramid, and this solid, as it stands on a support and with its bottom face concealed, presents eight faces and, as lifted from the support to expose all its faces, presents nine faces. Thus does the apron call attention to the Nine Significant Numbers, and hence, to the various philosophies of numbers.

Again, the solid suggested by the apron is the thurnel. The Broached Thurnel is, it is to be regretted, growing unfamiliar to many present-day Masons though it still appears upon the trestle board of the French Entered Apprentice. It is for the Entered Apprentice to try his Working Tools upon. Among English speaking Masons it has given place to the Perfect Ashlar.

Because of its shape--that of a rectangular parallelepiped surmounted by a rectangular pyramid - the solid suggested by the apron brings to mind the obelisks of Egypt. Thus the apron, by indirection, refers to the Pillars of the Porch, it being hardly open to question that those pillars found their suggestion in the obelisks erected, one at each side of the entrance, before Egyptian temples to symbolize the Northern and the Southern limit of the travel of the sun. From this point the student is led by an almost inappreciable step, to the consideration of Sun Worship, Circumambulation, the Egyptian Mysteries, the story of Osiris and his murder by Typhon and kindred matters.

The positions in which the apron is worn are also significant. Considering its position as a whole, it is worthy of notice that that position is about the waist. Being so placed the apron not only divides the human body into two distinct parts--the upper intellectual portion and the baser lower portion--but also, and what is of more importance, it conceals the lower portion. So, symbolically, it reveals the nobler qualities of Man and conceals the baser, always doing in theory that which it ought always to do in practice.

Considering the apron with regard to the varied positioning of the flap and the body in the first, the second, and the third degree, it is plan to be seen that the symbolism in this connection is identical with that of the Square and Compasses. That is, there is here symbolically presented the gradual domination of the Material represented by the Square, by the Spiritual, represented by the Triangle.

This final lesson--that Masonry inculcates the overcoming of the Material by the Spiritual--is the greatest teaching of the apron. Indeed, in giving us this crowning symbolism, does not this simple, white lambskin apron, presented to each of us in the period of our first gropings for Masonic Light, give us the summation of all the Teachings of Masonry?

Symbolism in the Apron

By J. George Gibson

The clothing of the Freemason is not introduced for the purpose of impressing "profanes", since it is almost entirely absent when the public is present. It is in the lodge functions alone that its use is compulsory, and the wearing of each article of Masonic clothing is but a memorial and a present signification of the Faith of a Mason. It is not only interesting, but it is essential to the effective life that the full significance of the apron should be realized by every Entered Apprentice, and remembered by those who from degree to degree go forward and upward to excellency and attainment.

For the institution of Modern Freemasonry in England we look to the seventeenth century; but for its origin and causation we may go back beyond Rosicrucianism and Essenism to the practice of the ancients of every age of worshippers. And, however far we travel we still find traces of the white lambskin apron as the clothing of Masonic novices. There must always have been some special significance connected with its use, and with the color also, as well as in its use. Indeed, it is upon these three lines of material, of color, and of user, that we must seek for light as to the full sense of its presentment to assembled brethren.

Attached to the idea of user are suggestions both of labor and of religion. From the earliest age of Noachidae there have been signs that labor and productive energy were, and would ever remain, honored by the highest distinction--because of their operative values. The Jewish, Persian and Egyptian dignitaries wore aprons to indicate their high rank. The royal standard of Persia, that land of fire worshippers, was originally an apron. And in the Ancient Mysteries of the Persian Mithras novices were clothed with white aprons, as also were others. And today certain dignitaries of churches are found wearing the apron, though of a somber color. In fact, Masonry appears through all ages to have been incorporated with the particular religions of each nation, and was to that body what religion is to theology.

Realizing that the builder is the true King of Man, the clothing of the operative builder was adopted by the speculative Freemason in the earliest age as the symbol of the priestly and teaching class. Nothing could so signify ability as could the dress of a workman, of a powerful operative of a builder of temples. And the consensus of today's millions approve the ancient dictum of the Sacred Law. Work is that which tells; and the clothing of a toiler is honorable above all other.

The color of a Mason's apron should be white. This is the color of light, the color that reflects most light, the clean color, which shows stains most plainly. It was the color worn by the Israelitish Levite, and by the later Essenes, by the Roman sacrificing priests, and by the Druid votaries of the highest degrees. The candidate for the Ancient Mysteries was clad in spotless white, and among Christian churches the officiating clergyman chiefly wears white while engaged in the sacred office.

White is the emblem of purity: and the Apocalyptic Seer, seeking to describe a Divine Justice as absolutely pure, tells us of the "great white throne of God", and of the purified as wearing robes of pure white. Is this not manifestly the reason why the Masonic novice is clothed with a pure white apron? Some Christian ministers clothe the candidates for baptism in white. Freemasonry receives her children to the white garb of purity. The Entered Apprentice has turned his back upon the "profane" world; and, when he passes the Tyler he is Masonically clad in purity and open to the impressions of Masonic life.

But, pure as the white light is, it is a composed color. It contains all the colors and is the perfected blend of colored lights. The Druid perhaps saw this when he made the last degree the white degree; and perhaps also the Roman priest knew this when in the supreme duty of his office he wore white in which to sacrifice. Certainly the Freemason acts wisely when he retains the white apron for the Entered Apprentice, since whatever that novice may become is already and only assured in the purity of his soul and desire as he takes the first Masonic steps.

Then the Masonic apron must be of simple lambskin. Not of cloth of gold, nor of rich silk, nor of a splendid texture of any kind. The lamb is the emblem of innocence, and of innocence sacrificed. All progress involves sacrifice and blood. If man would rise he must bleed somehow, or someone must. Primeval man's very raiment was the skin of slaughtered animals. Advance in civilization involves a victim; and the making of a Mason means a recognition of the cost of light and labor. In the highest degrees there are changes in form or in ornament. Perhaps the lambskin may be almost hidden under the red and blue of the Royal Arch, or by the jewels of rank and office: but the lambskin is there all the time, and a Masonic apron can be made properly of no other material. He who wears this is made conscious that as Cain built Enoch out of his loss and pain, so all Masons are compelled to prepare for the time when hard things are to be done, sore things to be endured, and fortitude to be cultivated. Masonry is not a mummery but a life; and the clothing of a Mason is that fit for his labor and suggestive of his duty.

And, lastly, the use of the lambskin apron symbolizes the great object of Freemasonry, the building of a Human Temple to the Great Architect of Heaven and earth. True, the blue strip of the craft color tells the virtue of Masonic brotherhood and trust, as well as the love which is over all and in all. But the ordinary white lambskin apron is much more eloquent could we realize all that it means.

I see a massive pile of Masonry before me in the ages long gone past. There are turban and bare heads, men of ranks and of all nations, fiery drabs and dark browed Gibeonites, active Tyrians and heavy limbed fellaheen from the banks of the river of Egypt. Some are but unskilled laborers; but many thousands wear the Mason's lambskin apron, and carry the tools of their calling. They are come from all lands to build a House for Jehovah, Solomon's God: and from the call to labor to the call off to refreshment they are hard at work. One is reducing the mighty blocks to shape, another is carefully squaring and smoothing the surface and making the even bed, another is carving the facade stones in chaste designs and obeying each command conveyed in the plans of the designers.

The scene changes. A weeping crowd of returned exiles cast off their garments and clear the level of the ancient ruins. These men also wear the apron of white lambskin. They have sacrificed and suffered, and suffer now. The same process and order and persistence. Again in scattered bands men gather upon the site of some Monastery, some fortress, some Cathedral, some Palace of Justice. There is the same white lambskin apron. There is the same obedience to the Master and there is the same loyalty to the Volume of the Sacred Law. The lambskin apron is the symbol of labor, of sacrifice, of construction, of obedience to design, of service to one's brothers, and of educative process ever going on.

We do not today stand alongside the rude mason's bench and with gavel and chisel dress huge blocks of hardest stone. But we stand before a delicately adjusted masterpiece, which we must finish, or fail in our lives. The world is our workshop; the tools of a mason are in our hands, and the apron is both speculative and operative in suggestion. We are called to cultivate character, to deepen human sympathy, to draw closer the chords of brotherly love, and to prepare ourselves by discipline for each post as the great Grand Master shall appoint us. We have before us imperfect Human Society, which must be saved by progress, and established by the inspiration of a Humanity, which includes, but is greater than patriotism. The reminder of the Mason's apron ought to inspire us to a nobler consecration and a more human interest and service. We must wear it, in lodge, until we are called of labor, and the hour of our Eternal Rest is come, and the voice of the Great Warden calls us home.

The Altar of Freemasonry

By William Harvey

The enthusiastic Freemason who is genuinely interested in the system of morality which the Order exists to inculcate climbs rung after rung of the ladder which leads to knowledge in our mystic circle. Doubtless the brother who reaches the summit forgets much that he has learned in the course of his toilsome ascent, but one thing he is ever likely to remember is the Altar at which he knelt as an Initiate, and upon which, when darkness had been removed from his wondering eyes, he beheld the three great Lights of our Ancient and Honorable Fraternity. The Altar is the rallying point of Masonic thought. It is the point with the Masonic circle at which all distinctions among men are swept away, and to which every member may stand related in a common endeavor to achieve a splendid equality of Virtue, Morality, and Brotherly Love. Rising from this sacred spot at which, by his belief in God and his honor as a man, he has pledged himself to secrecy, fidelity, and obedience, the young mason is privileged to view the Lodge as an emblem of the Universe, and to note the symbols of the Faith of which, of his own free will and accord, he has become a devotee. And the Altar itself may first claim his attention.

From earliest days the Altar has been invested with peculiarly sacred associations, and in most religions has been regarded as an indispensable requisite of every place of worship. In primitive times it was believed to be the temporary abode of the Deity; and, if the idea is well founded that the

Lodge is a symbol of the Universe, it is fitting that the Altar should occupy a central position since the Supreme Being, whose favor we solicit, and whose love we acknowledge, is the center and source of all creation. The original purpose of an altar was to provide a place where sacrifices could be made. After the erection of the Tabernacle, there was added the Altar of incense which is described as square in section, one cubit each way, and two cubits in height, with projecting horns; and authorities insist that that is the proper form of a Masonic Altar. In the Jewish ritual the Altar had a three-fold significance: it was the place where sacrifices were made, where incense was offered, and at its horns certain classes of offenders found sanctuary. In modern Freemasonry, the whole may be moralized as the spot at which the fervent Craftsman offers the incense of Brotherly Love, Relief, and Truth, on which he lays unruly passions and worldly appetites as a fitting sacrifice to the genius of the Order, and under the shadow of which he finds sanctuary from greed, and avarice, and other lusts that would devour him.

The Altar is the appropriate resting-place of the three great Lights of Masonry which are the Volume of the Sacred Law, the Square, and the Compasses. These are called the furniture of the Lodge, and are dedicated respectively to God, to the Master, and to the Craft. The Initiate is told that the Bible is a gift from God to man to rule and govern his faith, the Square is to square his actions, and the Compasses to keep him in due bounds with all mankind. Oliver, in his lectures, illustrates the three Lights as follows :- "The Bible", he says, "is said to derive from God to man in general, because the

Almighty has been pleased to reveal more of His divine will by that holy Book than by any other means. The Compasses, being the chief implement used in the construction of all architectural plans and designs, are assigned to the Grand Master in particular, as emblems of His dignity, He being the chief Head and Ruler of the Craft. The Square is given to the whole Masonic body, because we are all obligated within it, and are consequently bound to act thereon." As we rise from the Altar to take our place in the Universe symbolized in the Lodge we, as worthy Masons, should carry the three great Lights with us, letting them be lamps unto our feet in all our later days: treasuring in our hearts the Volume of the Sacred Law as the unerring standard of Truth, the Square as the monitor of mercy, and the Compasses as the symbol of that circle of Temperance in all things by which we should constantly surround ourselves.

Passing from the Altar and the Lights, the Initiate may next observe the form of the Lodge of which he is now a unit. It is what is popularly, if somewhat inaccurately, described as "an oblong square", and is situated due east and west. According to Oliver the form of the lodge ought to be "a double cube expressive of the united powers of darkness and light in the creation, and because the ark of the Covenant and the Altar of incense were both of that figure." Dr. Albert G. Mackey, in his 'Lexicon of Freemasonry," puts forward the theory that the oblong form has a symbolic allusion to the ancient world. "If," he says, "we draw lines which shall circumscribe just that portion of the world which was known and inhabited at the time of the building of Solomon's Temple, these lines, running a short distance north and south of the

Mediterranean Sea, and extending from Spain to Asia Minor, will form an oblong square, whose greatest length will be from east to west, and whose greatest breadth will be from north to south. This oblong square, he adds, which thus enclosed the whole inhabited part of the globe would represent the form of the Lodge, to denote the universality of Masonry, since the world constitutes the Lodge; a doctrine that has since been taught in that expressing sentence: In every clime the Mason may find a home, and in every land a brother." Brethren with a larger imagination take even a broader view than Mackey, telling us that the Lodge represents the whole universe, being in length from east to west, and in breadth from north to south, and in height even to Heaven itself. And it is just because of this that the roof is frequently decorated to represent the starry firmament, an emblem of those immortal mansions to which faithful Masons hope at last to ascend, there to behold the Grand Master of the Universe who reigns forever. To reach the celestial city the Initiate is taught that he must climb a ladder which rests upon the Volume of the Sacred Law, and of which the principal rungs are Faith, Hope and Charity — Faith in God, Hope of Immortality, and Charity towards all men.

The Ladder, frequently called Jacob's Ladder, because it suggests that which appeared to Jacob in his vision at Bethel, is one of the prominent emblems of the Tracing Board to which the Initiate's attention may next be directed. There is a tradition that in early days the speculative Mason, anxious to illustrate his teaching, followed the fashion of his Operative brother, and chalked the desired design on the floor of the Lodge, just as today, in rural places, we may find a stonemason who draws upon the ground the arch for which he is dressing stones. It is probably on account of this ancient custom that one prominent feature in the movable Tracing-Board of today is what is called the Mosaic Pavement which represent the Floor or Carpet of the Lodge.

The pavement itself with its checkered squares is a fit emblem of human life, with all its lights and shadows - its joys and sorrows, its successes and failures. Today "our feet tread in prosperity, tomorrow we totter on the uneven paths of weakness, temptation and adversity," and, therefore, by such a moral emblem as this we are taught "not to boast of anything but to give heed to our ways, and walk with humility and uprightness before God."

The Pavement is skirted by the indented or Tessellated Border, and the whole is bound by a cord of sixty threads which terminate in tassels pendant from the corners. The conventional explanation of the Indented Border is, that, as the Pavement "points out to us the diversity of objects which decorate and adorn the whole creation," so the Border "refers us to the Planets which, in their various revolutions, form a beautiful border or skirt-work round the Sun," an explanation which, I fear, is not very satisfactory. A more reasonable interpretation is given of the cord of sixty strands. These strands, Bro. J.G. Gibson tells us, "represent the regular number of members" that were wont to be in a Lodge, and the whole, he adds, "was arranged round the boards with a series of lovers' knots - all meaning the mystic tie by which each of the members of the Lodge, and all, might be regarded as bound to serve the brotherhood and each member of it."

The Tassels pendant from the corners are called the Guttural, Pectoral, Manual and Pedal Tassels, and they allude to the four Cardinal Points of the Lodge — N. S. E. and W. — the four Cardinal Virtues, and the Mason who desires a Biblical reference says that they also refer to the four rivers of Paradise. According to one authority they point us to four deliberate acts in the First Degree: -

Guttural, the tongue, alludes to the penalty of the Obligation under which the Initiate swore never to divulge the secrets of the Order; Pectoral, the breast, in which the Freemason safely deposits his secrets from a curious world; Manual, the hand placed on the Volume of the Sacred law, as a testimony of his assent o the Obligation of a Mason; and Pedal, the feet placed in the form of a Square at the N.E. part of the Lodge to denote a just and upright man and Mason.

Another authority connects the four more closely with the Cardinal Virtues and that as follows: -

Guttural, belonging to the throat; and as the throat is that avenue of the body which is most employed in the sins of excessive indulgence, it suggest to the Mason symbolic instructions in relation to the virtue of Temperance; Pectoral, belonging to the breast; and as the heart has always been considered the seat of fortitude and courage, the word suggest to the Mason certain symbolic instructions in relation to the virtue of Fortitude; Manual, belonging to the hand, and as in a peculiar manner masons are reminded by the hand of the necessity of a prudent and careful observance of all their pledges and duties, therefore this organ suggests certain symbolic instructions in relation to the virtue of Prudence; and Pedal, belong to the feet and therefore, as a just man is he who plants his feet on the solid foundation of right, and cannot be moved from that position either by the allurements of flattery, or the frowns of arbitrary power, so the word suggests to the Mason certain symbolic instructions in relation to the virtue of Justice.

It is a pious belief, indicating boundless charity of mind, that the Cardinal Virtues which are indicated on the Tracing Board by the Tassels were constantly practiced by a great majority of our ancient brethren; and whether that be so or not, there cannot be any manner of doubt but that the Mason of today who seeks to regulate his daily life and conduct by them will not only be a worthy and valued member of society, but a faithful brother of our ancient and honorable Fraternity.

Still keeping in view that the Lodge is a symbol of the Universe, and that the Universe is the Temple of the Supreme Being who we acknowledge as Master, the student of the Tracing Board may next be directed to observe the three Pillars that are grouped around the Altar. These great Pillars are symbols of the supports of the Lodge and the Universe, and represent Wisdom, Strength, and Beauty, the divine attributes of Him whose Wisdom is infinite, whose Strength is omnipotent, and whose Beauty shines throughout the whole of creation in symmetry and order. Moralizing upon the Pillars and the attributes they symbolize, the meditative Mason learns that he should strive to acquire. Wisdom to guide him in all the undertakings of this life, supplicate Strength to support him in all times of difficulty, and cultivate that Beauty of holiness which will enable him to adorn the inward man with faith in God and hope of an immortal land, where the dreams of our present earth will be realized in fullest measure.

The other outstanding features of the first Tracing Board are the Ashlars and the movable Jewels, all of which are intimately related to each other in our system of morality. The rough Ashlar is a symbol of man in his rude and ignorant condition uninfluenced by education or other refining process, but, just as the unhewn stone from the quarry is, by the industry and skill of the Operative, wrought into due form and rendered suitable for the most elegant building, so man, by the tender care and wise instruction of those around him is educated, refined and made a fit member of civilized society. Thus improved, and living constantly by the Square of God's Word and Compasses of a good conscience, man becomes a subject who may be fitly illustrated by that symbol which we call the Perfect Ashlar. In transforming the stone from its rough to its polished state the movable Jewels — Square, Level and Plumb-rule - are employed and consequently each has its distinct place in Masonic allegory. The Square is a constant reminder to the freemason that he should regulate his action by the Masonic rule and line which are laid down in the volume of the Sacred Law, and that he should never forget that, just as the stone is tried and proved by the application of the Square, so, by the application of the eternal and unchanging principles of morality, each action in human life is judged, and its value ascertained. The Level is an emblem of the equality of all men in the sight of the Eternal God who will reward or punish us, not according as we may have gained or lost the things that belong to this world, but according as we have obeyed or disregarded His divine commands. The Plumb-rule is the symbol of justness and uprightness of life and action and admonishes the Freemason to walk with humility before God and ever to have eternity in view.

The lessons that the faithful and earnest Craftsman learns at the Altar of Freemasonry, and from a study of the Tracing board, must lead him instinctively to recognize that the distinguishing characteristics of the Brotherhood are Virtue, Honor and Mercy.

It is said that Marcellus, the roman consul, contemplated building a temple to Virtue and Honor, but departed from the idea, and later, erected two structures so placing them that the worshipper who desired to approach the temple of Honor could only do so by passing through the temple of Virtue. The design of the Consul is object lesson to all men that Honor cannot be attained except by Virtue. To make men virtuous is one of the main objects of the Fraternity. Virtue has been described as the highest exercise of Reason, and Honor as the most manly sentiment or impulse of the soul which Virtue can inspire. The actions of all good men are regulated by Honor, for the man of Honor scorns to do evil. The Virtuous and the Honorable man is also a man of Mercy, that quality which adds luster to the monarch's crown, freshness to the victor's wreath, and is the chief attribute of the deity on whom the best and wisest of men must rest his hope when the actions of this mortal life are weighed in the eternal balance.

Virtue, Honor, and Mercy crown the hill of high endeavor which every faithful craftsman seeks to climb, and if he be true to his code, and earnest in his toil, then, in the words of the familiar lecture, "though these characteristics should be banished from all other societies they will still be found in a Mason's breast."

The lessons which the Freemason learns at the Altar would not only be seen reflected in his own life, but should help him to influence the world around. The thought is beautifully expressed in the opening lines of a poems by br. McBride, Bard of Leven St. John No. 1 70:—

Go forth, go forth and be a Mason true

    Be master of thyself, and thou shalt sway

A mightier scepter than great Caesar knew,

    A Kingdom grander, born not for a day,

But as thyself - - immortal.

The Altar

By H. L. Haywood

I

In the center of the lodge stands the Altar. It should be cubical in shape, and about three feet in height, and it should have horns at each corner to suggest, in light of a hoary usage, that it is a place of refuge. On the East, the South, and the West should be placed one of the representatives of the three Lesser Lights, but never on the North, for that is the place of darkness. On its top, in due arrangement, should lie the three Grand Lights. Thus arranged it may well be considered "the most important article of furniture in a lodge room," and the ground whereon it stands as "the most holy place." Too universal in its use, both through space and time, to admit of our tracing its history here we must content ourselves with some reference to the ideas embodied in it. To this end let us remember, here and everywhere, that the Masonic life is not that which occurs in the lodge rooms alone, for that is but its allegorical picture, its tracing-board; but it is that which a Mason should do and be in all circumstances, under the inspiration of the Fraternity and its teachings. Thus understood the Altar standing in the center of the Masonic lodge is the symbol of something that must operate at the center of the Masonic life.

Often serving as a table whereon the worshipper may lay his gifts to God, the Altar may well remind us of the necessity of that human gratitude which leads us to return to Him the gifts He has showered upon us. This

is that teaching of stewardship found in all religions to remind us that our very lives are not our own, having been bought with a price, and that our talents are held in trusteeship to be rendered again to Him to whom they belong. Thus stated, I know, the matter may sound bald and even unappealing, but once we encounter a man who lives his life as a stewardship held in the frail tenure of the flesh, we see to what high issues the character of man may ascend; such personalities carry an atmosphere about with them as of another world, and radiate influences that are light and fragrant. Surely, a man who denied this in his practices can never serve as a living Building Stone in Masonry's Temple!

II

In its proper sense also the Altar serves as a sanctuary, a place of refuge, and this too has much to tell us, though I am aware of the dangers of moralizing. In the earlier centuries of our era, before the complete development of common law, the hunted criminal, fleeing from his pursuers, would escape to a church and there lay hold of the horns of the Altar; in that he found safety, and an opportunity to prove his innocence, if innocent he was. Out of this arose the beautiful customs of "sanctuary," the chivalrous unselfish harboring of the weak, the sorrowful, and the afflicted. Is there not a sanctuary in Masonry? Certainly there is, for in the Fraternity itself, in the privacy of its inner fellowships, a brother will often find rest for his heart and relief from the bruisings of the world; and a man is no true Mason in whose nature there is not at least one inner chamber in which the weary may find rest and the weak may have protection.

More than a table for gifts and a place of sanctuary the Altar has from of old served as the station of sacrifice, and this usage also is recognized in our symbolism, for therein we are taught that the human in us, our appetites, our passions, yea our life itself if need be, must be laid down in the service of man and the glory of God. How otherwise could Masonry remain Masonry if it is "the subjugation of the human that is in man, by the Divine?"

III

Of the Altar as a place of prayer we have already spoken, but in this connection we may well ponder a paragraph from Dr. J. F. Newton, composed of those lucid sentences of which he is a master:

"Thus by a necessity of his nature man is ever a seeker after God, touched at times with a strange sadness and longing, and laying aside his tools to look out over the far horizon. Whatever else he may have been—vile, tyrannous, vindictive—the story of his long search after God is enough to prove that he is not wholly base. Rites horrible, and even cruel, may have been a part of his early ritual, but if the history of past ages had left us nothing but the memory of a race at prayer, they would have left us rich. And so, following the good custom of the great ones of former ages, we gather at our Altar lifting up hands in prayer, moved thereto by the ancient need and aspiration of our humanity. Like the man who walked in the grey years of old, our need is for God, the living God, whose presence hallows all our mortal life, even to its last ineffable homeward sigh which men call death."

www.ingramcontent.com/pod-product-compliance
Lightning Source LLC
LaVergne TN
LVHW041500070426
835507LV00009B/707